a gift for

_____

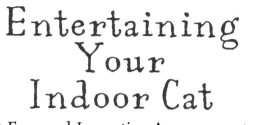

Entertaining Your Indoor Cat

25 Fun and Inventive Amusements for Your Cat

KEVIN P. KELLY

Illustrations by Wendy Crowell

SELLERS
PUBLISHING

Published by Sellers Publishing, Inc.
161 John Roberts Road, South Portland, ME 04106
Visit us at www.sellerspublishing.com • E-mail: rsp@rsvp.com

Copyright © 2015 Kevin P. Kelly
Illustrations © 2015 Wendy Crowell

ISBN-13: 978-1-4162-4550-6

Printed and bound in China.

10 9 8 7 6 5 4 3 2 1

Contents

Introduction

Welcome to the new, concise edition of *Entertaining Your Indoor Cat*. If you are a fan of the first, somewhat furrier, edition of the book, you will undoubtedly enjoy this one as well. Contained within these smaller, action-packed pages of fun feline activities are some old favorites and a few new tricks, all approved by my personal activity testers — Forrest, Pie, and Butter (ages 14, 12, and 8, respectively) — who remain firmly committed to their indoor lifestyle, believing, as do I, that it is the best choice to ensure a kitty's good health and longevity.

I have enjoyed hearing from many of the readers of *Entertaining Your Indoor Cat*, and I greatly appreciate your useful suggestions. Thanks to all of my fellow cat lovers who took the time not only to write to me, but to play and interact with their kitties each day. For this edition, I've included the best of the best and combined top cat picks with readers' choices to create a volume I hope will provide hours of crazy cat fun for readers and their feline friends.

Readers of this book will also enjoy the updates to the delightfully playful illustrations by Wendy Crowell, who added lovely hand coloring to some of her original work.

As always, I look forward to hearing from readers and cat lovers, and I am happy to receive comments, ideas, and suggestions. My e-mail cat door remains open at kkindoorcat@gmail.com, so feel free to contact me to say hi or meow, and let me know how much fun your own crazy kitties are having.

ENTERTAINING KITTENS

Kittens start actively playing when they are around three to four weeks old. At that age, the adorable puff balls begin to try out their stalking skills, pouncing and grabbing items and delivering little death-blow kicks with their back paws. These playful moves may actually be hunting techniques they're instinctively developing at an early age. Of course, they may also just be fooling around and burning up all that kitten energy, like any toddler riding in circles in the backyard on a clattering plastic Big Wheel. Whatever the reason, once kittens reach that certain age, they need and enjoy playtime with other kittens and with their human companions.

The following games for kittens are gentle fun for your baby mouser who's just beginning to learn the ropes and is starting to flex his claws and muscles.

Later in this section, you'll discover all sorts of rough 'n' tumble, dynamic activities your older kittens and adult cats will enjoy. For now, if you have very young kittens, your best bet is to keep things simple. Let them gently discover the world of play as they learn how much fun they can have interacting with their human companions.

swat, swish, clutch & stare:
playtime for your kitten

Kittens, like all toddlers, are delighted by and curious about all sorts of ordinary things. Often the simplest items provide these playful, fuzzy tykes with the greatest entertainment. Strings and ribbons and other fascinating objects that kittens can swat, stare at, or clutch and hold can supply an eager young kitty with a variety of mesmerizing moments. With a little imagination, which kittens have in abundance, these simple activities allow for hours of giddy feline fun guaranteed to brighten any kitty's day.

CAUTION: Any small bits of material can be hazardous to a cat or kitten's health. Be careful not to let your homemade toys shred or break unless you're prepared to dispose of them right away. Cats and kittens shouldn't be allowed to swallow this type of material, but given the opportunity, they may do so. Have fun — but be careful and always take care to watch out for your cat's safety.

Yo-Yo Mouse

Even if you've never been a master of the yo-yo, this is a game that's sure to get your hyper kitten's attention.

A mouse goes up, a mouse goes down, and your kitten tries to grab it. The trick is keeping the stuffed mouse away from your kitten's lightning paws.

This game might be more of a challenge for you: Who's faster — you or your kitten?

What You'll Need
- A piece of strong string, about two feet long
- A generous supply of fat, plush mice

How It Works

Dangle a soft, stuffed mouse, which you've secured to the end of a string, in front of your eager kitten. Jerk the mouse up, and then drop it down, always just out of kitty's reach. You control the action with a flick of the wrist, right before your kitten's nose.

Kittens can't resist the fast, darting action you create by popping the string and making the mouse leap and twirl elusively. Then let the mouse dangle, tantalizingly, in front of the kitten's nose. Kitty'll play possum, but so will you. Be ready to jerk the string up when you see her paw flash out as she tries to nab that annoying mouse. And every so often, let her win. After all, she's just a kitten.

Phishing

If you have ever had to catch a fish without any gear, you'll know that the old-fashioned art of hooking one can be done with a simple, improvised hook and some bait. Phishing is that kind of game, except the gear includes a length of string and a small, soft toy as the "bait." Kittens and their human pals can have lots of fun, whether they're fisher-folks or not. Play this one, and you'll develop a bit of the angler's skill yourself, trying to land your kitten.

What You'll Need

- A length of strong string, about two to three feet long (The dangling action is harder to manage with longer pieces.)
- Lightweight, small, fabric novelty bugs to use as bait, or even a sprig of fresh catnip — if you have access to some

How It Works

Trot out your trusty length of string. Tie your novelty bug or even a treat (a large, soft Pounce will do the trick) to the end. Next, flick your string/knot combo toward kitty and see if she takes the bait. See how close you can land the knot to her paw, and then pull it away across the floor and watch her chase it.

Pole Fishin'

A variation of Phishing, this game requires a higher skill level — you have to master the art of "fly" flicking while using a pole. But this can be a fun challenge for you and an entertaining interlude for your kitten.

What You'll Need
- A thin garden stake or plastic kitty-toy wand, about 30 to 36 inches long
- A suitable length of flickable string
- A small plastic bug or toy as "bait"

How It Works

As in traditional Phishing, you'll enjoy mastering the art of the flick; however, your wrist action here is closer to the traditional fly-fishing technique you've, perhaps, always dreamed about perfecting. Now the pole has become an extension of your wrist — you will become one with the soft bug at the end of the line — a Zen master of kitty fishing.

So, maybe you're not decked out in hip waders, battling a trophy trout in the middle of the Yellowstone River. Your kitten will still be mighty impressed by Mom's or Dad's fishing prowess.

The object of the game remains the same: Land the bait near the target zone and watch your kitten grab it.

After securing your string to the end of the pole, start casting your fly around your kitten. Try landing the fly near various toys, under a chair, or on a table. Drag the fly across the floor and let kitty race after it.

Rodeo Mouse & Cowboy Kitten!

Yee-haw! Round 'em up! Time to pull on your cowboy boots and smooth the crease in your Stetson. The rodeo has come to town, and your kitten's the star attraction.

It appears that the mice have been strayin' again, pardner, and your kitten's got to get busy and round 'em all up.

What You'll Need
- Six to ten stuffed mice tied to long pieces of string
- An open-topped cardboard box to use as your holding pen, with four arch-shaped mouse holes — one on each side
- Optional gear: mini cowboy hat, boots, kitty chaps, bandanna

How It Works

Assemble a large herd of toy mice in your rodeo holding pen (a small cardboard box, with cut-out mouse holes, works nicely for this purpose).

Make sure each mouse has been lassoed with a good length of string before you place the mice in their pen. Make sure your kitten is watching. Next, begin pulling on the strings, moving each mouse out of the pen and across the floor.

If your kitten is alert, he'll pounce before the mouse gets too far — but wait, another one's coming! Pretty soon the whole herd will be movin' out as you pull the strings in different directions. Your kitten won't know which way to turn as he pounces here and there, trying to contain the errant mice.

On, no! Saddle up, Cowboy Kitty! They're headin' fer the river!

Catnip Pull

Here's another string-chase game, with the irresistible lure of catnip thrown in for a bonus. Cats always love to sniff, lick, and roll in the 'nip, but this game makes them work for it. Hey, before you know it, they're going to get hooked on the wacky weed anyway. You may as well introduce them to the good stuff.

What You'll Need
- A suitable length of string
- A bag of catnip (Be choosy about your catnip, select a premium grade.)
- A selection of stuffable toys with plastic zippers or Velcro closures
- A selection of catnip-filled toys (optional)

How It Works

Roll out your reliable string and tie the catnip-filled toy on securely. Now drag the toy along the floor, tantalizing your kitten. Make it stop, then go, let it wiggle and twirl, and watch your kitty go wild.

Hide it under a chair or an ottoman, and watch her try to grab it. If you're up to it (and your hallways can take it), jog through the house, pulling the string behind you. Your kitten will be after you and the toy like a shot, racing along the floor, stalking and pouncing.

As always, make sure you let kitty score some satisfying wins, and allow her the chance to savor the sweet taste and smell of victory.

Pinwheel on a Stick

Movement of any kind fascinates cats and turns on their hunting instinct. Kittens, of course, are just discovering and developing their stalking skills, but like their adult counterparts, they love to watch things flicker and move.

What You'll Need
- A plastic pinwheel (available at most novelty or toy stores)
- A small table fan — if you're feeling breathless
- A plastic flowerpot filled with sand, dirt, or a Styrofoam florist's block

How It Works

Like the other fascination games described here, this one doesn't require your kitten to do much except pay attention — and maybe space out. Gather your plastic pinwheel, the flowerpot, or whatever you'll use as a stand for the pinwheel. If using option two, place the pinwheel securely in the stand of choice.

   Option one: Hold the pinwheel in front of the kitten, blow on the blades, and the pinwheel twirls.

   Option two: Use a small table fan to do the work for you. Set the fan on low, then sit back to watch. Note: The electric fan makes supervision mandatory for this activity.

   Option three: Set up the pinwheel outside in a window flower box, so the wind catches the blades. Let kitten sit in the window and watch — if the sun is shining on the blades, a light show becomes part of the action.

I'm Forever Chasing Bubbles

Okay, kitties! Time for your bubble bath!

Ha. Fat chance. No self-respecting kitten would ever voluntarily take that plunge, but bubbles are another story.

What You'll Need
- Bubble solution and a blowing wand
- Sufficient lung power to blow bubbles

How It Works

Dip your wand in the bubble bottle, then carefully pull the wand out of the bottle and blow. You can also wave your wand through the air, letting a stream of smaller bubbles float out behind you.

Sure, that sounds like fun for you, but what does the kitten get out of it? The bubbles, of course, delight cats, too.

Some kitties like to pounce when the bubbles are within striking distance; others prefer simply to stare and follow the path of the bubble, waiting for it to land gently on the floor.

Try blowing bubbles of various sizes and shapes, or treat your kitty to a trip back in time. Pick up a bottle of catnip-flavored bubble solution, designed especially for kitties. Cats love the aroma, of course, and they'll have twice as much fun, sniffing and watching all the cool sizes and shapes drifting into the air.

So let your kitten groove on bubbles, man! Toss in a catnip kick and turn on the Moody Blues — she'll be partying like it's 1969!

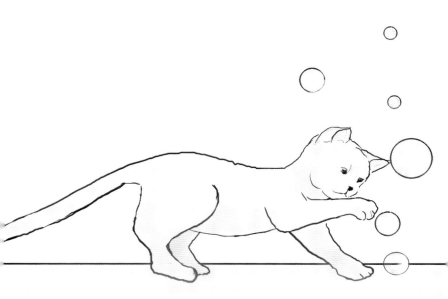

Birdies Through a Window

Your kitten probably has already figured this one out on her own, but just in case the outside action is a little slow, you can keep kitty on her toes and encourage your feathered friends to drop by for a visit.

What You'll Need
- Birdseed! Yes, that's what will lure those chickadees, sparrows, and robins to fly and flutter in front of the window.
- A kitty cushion or window perch

How It Works

Set up a bird feeder, if you don't have one in your yard already, and fill it with your favorite birdseeds. You can also simply spread the seed out on the lawn or on the railing of your deck.

Set up a nice viewing area for your kitten and invite (or place) him in front of the window once the birds start to arrive. The neighborhood birds will send out the signal that dinner is served, and your fluttering guests will congregate outside the window.

Guaranteed your kitten will enjoy the show — at least until the birdseed runs out. And he won't want to change the channel.

Rassle the Tassel

What's more tempting than a bushy-tailed squirrel? Well, a simple-to-make fluttering tassel may be just the answer.

What You'll Need

- A large pincushion (without the pins, of course) or small novelty pillow (Sewing-supply stores are good sources.)
- Dangling materials to enhance your tassel: ribbons, string, or whatever works tc cover the cushion

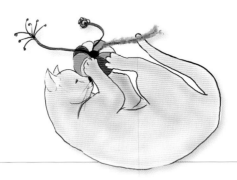

How It Works

You'll be tempting (okay, taunting) your kitten with a fat, soft, wiggly lump, and the object is to get kitty to pounce, then work her claw-clutch magic.

You'll need something that's eye-catching yet annoying enough to raise your kitten's hackles. A plump little pillow or a large pincushion serves the purpose nicely. But to make it attractive enough to earn kitty's claws, you'll have to get creative. Cover the pincushion with dangling strings or ribbons, attached securely with thread or nontoxic "superglue." Attach a long string from the center so you can dangle the object, and now you've got a giant tassel.

Try dangling it in front of your kitten or dragging it across the floor. Let the ribbons tickle her belly and ears or flutter in front of her face — you're not playing keep-away; you want your kitten to catch it. If the object is the right size, kitty will grab it and dig in, kicking her back feet and curling her body around the tassel.

Try moving it while she has it in her clutches — she'll work even harder, making sure it doesn't get away. And if you make a few tassels of different sizes and shapes, you'll keep kitty interested in this game, instead of in the sofa and the carpets.

Kitten Caboose

Turn your playroom or hallway into a Kitty-Kiddie Park as you take your little engineer for a ride on the Rug-Train Express.

What You'll Need
- An old scatter rug or carpet remnant, suitable for pulling
- A room or a hallway with a smooth floor to serve as your track
- Matching Casey Jones caps for you and your kitty (optional)
- All the bells and whistles

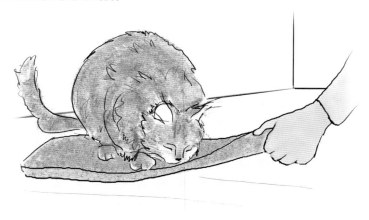

How It Works

We all remember the thrill of our first ride on an amusement park's miniature train. There we were, sitting proudly in our seats, waving as Mom and Dad cheered us on, the tiny train chugging along past fake windmills and railroad depots, tooting its eardrum-piercing whistle and grinding to a sudden halt after a kid fell off the back.

Well, now your kitten can experience the same joy and excitement you did as a child.

First, get her attention with a *toot! toot!* whistle sound and begin pulling your scatter rug down the hall. When kitty's ready to play, she'll hop aboard and hang on for the ride. Pull her slowly (you don't want to lose her) up and down the hall or around the room. Keep tooting or making a cool chugging sound as your rug train clatters along, with Kitten Caboose bringing up the rear, flicking her tail with delight.

Cats love to glide around the room with their humans providing the power. Once kitty gets the hang of this one, she'll start the action, and when she wants to play, she'll be waiting for you at the station, sitting on the rug, ready for you to shovel the coal and fire up the engine.

All aboard!

ADULT ENTERTAINMENT

Now that your kitty is all grown up, it's time for you and Mr. Mature to enjoy more sophisticated entertainment. Face it: he's not a clinging kitten anymore — heck, by now he's probably moved into his own kitty condo — so it's time to engage his interest with new and challenging activities that will keep him active, alert, and in top cat shape.

It's a good idea to participate in active playtime with your indoor cat for about 15 minutes, two or three times a day. If you play a few of the games listed here each day, you'll look forward to these play sessions with the same enthusiasm as kitty. Then you'll both be tuckered out, Mr. Mature will be satisfied, and you won't feel guilty snoozing with him on the sofa for the rest of the evening.

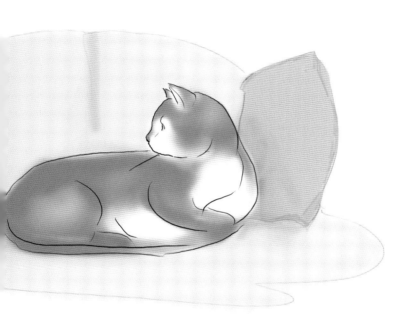

digitize, aerobicize & keep your grown-up kitty moving

The various games and activities in this section are designed to keep your adult cat friend healthy, happy, monomaniacally intrigued, and/or completely spaced-out staring at ridiculous things.

Workout activities and feline sports are essential for an indoor cat's good health, and several of the games in this section are designed to keep your bustling bundle of fur movin', groovin', and healthy. For techno-savvy millennial mewers, the gadget games included here offer plenty of opportunities for your adult tabby to experience the same mind-numbing, mesmeric joy we humans have been indulging in for the past 40-plus years. And as much as we enjoy tickling kitty's fuzzy gut when she's on her back, none of us wants to experience a painful hand or arm shredding. So, here you will also find a few safety tips and sneaky tricks to help you, beloved human, avoid the razor claws of your lovingly playful mouser.

Mouse Toss!

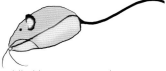

Relive your glory days of shootin' hoops while kitty gets a workout.

What You'll Need
- A basket, a bag, or a cardboard box, deep enough to keep the mice from bouncing out
- A good supply of soft, stuffed mice. The fatter ones work best for this game.

How It Works

This game requires a bit of skill from both you and your cat.

The idea is for you to toss stuffed mice into a container (any box, basket, or bag will do) placed several feet across the room. Kitty's job is to block the shot and/or go after the mice that have either landed in the basket for a score (Three points! Why not?) or skidded across the floor after you've shot an airball.

The scoring is simple: three points for you for each shot you make; three points for the cat if she blocks it.

One of our cats has caught on to this game, and they enjoy the challenge. He waits for the shot, blocks it like a pro, and usually ends up winning, displaying his pleasure with the kitty equivalent of the high five: tail up, smug and sassy.

Calorie burn? Hard to measure, but this game definitely keeps our Maine Coon active.

Crazy Susan

Make this spinning food-delivery device an essential piece of exercise equipment for your aerobically active kitty.

What You'll Need
- A good variety of intriguing toys — all shapes, styles, and sizes
- A sturdy plastic or wooden Lazy Susan, available at most kitchen stores
- A few tasty treats (optional)

How It Works

Place your Lazy Susan on the floor and arrange a tempting selection of toys on top of the wheel. Variety is the spice of this lively game, so mix in fresh catnip sacks, plush mice, balls, and wispy feathers. If kitty's not on a serious diet, add a few treats (we'll call them cat power bars) to the wheel.

Once the toys are arranged, let the fun begin. Start spinning the Lazy Susan, slowly at first, as your cat watches the toys and treats whirling around and around. She may try to swat them off the wheel, or she may try to pounce. Either way, she'll be after those toys, and chances are, the toys will soon be airborne.

As kitty gets used to the spinning wheel, try moving it a little faster. Cats enjoy staring, then pouncing, as the wheel turns around. Your cat may even try moving the Lazy Susan herself. However cats choose to engage with this game, they'll be active, alert, and workin' out.

Power to the kitties!

Ping-Pong Paws

Every executive cat enjoys a brisk workout at the club after a hard day of mousing. This game gives your mighty mouse-winner a chance to unwind (and lose some weight) after a long day in the carpeted jungle.

What You'll Need

- A bathtub
- Ping-pong balls

How It Works

The playing court is your own clean, dry bathtub. A deeper tub makes it easier to keep the ball in play — and to keep your kitty moving.

Step one is to remove all obstacles from the tub: soap, conditioner, your rubber duck — anything that will slow kitty down or interfere with the ball's movement.

Once you and your cat are ready to play, place kitty (never force him, of course) in the bathtub. Toss a ping-pong ball in the air or bounce it off the wall to ramp up the excitement. Then throw it in the tub and let it bounce. Your cat will go after it, trying to trap it with his claws. Since ping-pong balls are hard to grasp (at least, if you don't have thumbs), the ball and cat will keep moving. If the game starts to slow down, throw in another ball or two and watch things get really wild. The balls will bounce and roll around the tub, careening off the sides and popping into the air as your cat goes after them, scrambling and leaping.

Scoring? Nah — it's a workout game. If you want to keep your cat happy and svelte, try this game; it's one he'll want to keep on playing.

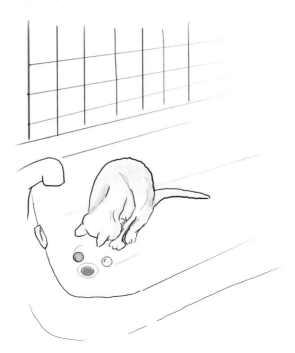

Ice-Cube Hockey

Heads up! Kitty's on the ice, armed with a vicious slapshot.

What You'll Need
- A bowl of ice
- A cardboard box to serve as the net
- A floor with a smooth surface and plenty of room
- Painter's tape (optional)

How It Works

The rules are similar to a real hockey game: For each goal, you score a point. Of course, like most games you play with your cat, there really aren't any rules, and if there were, your cat would change them.

First, set up your hockey rink, establishing goal lines, a center line, and boundaries with your painter's tape. Don't worry about regulation specs — with this game, the more floor space you have, the better. Establish two goal areas at either end of the room. Your cardboard box, cut in half, will serve as your goal nets.

Start the game by placing an ice-cube puck on the center line, then flicking it with your finger toward a goal. Kitty will pounce at the slippery cube and knock it back toward you or against the wall, or maybe even toward your goal.

You and your cat can take turns playing offense and defense and acting as goalie. Either way, once you put the ice puck in play, your cat will be actively engaged. Now it's your turn to take a whack at the cube and try to send it past kitty. See if you can score a goal — but don't get overconfident; cats are excellent defenders. And your cat may surprise you, scoring a few goals himself. (Cats, of course, are famous for their hat tricks.)

The object, sort of, is to score goals, but you'll both have fun just knocking the ice cube around the floor. When it melts down to a small size, bring out a fresh cube and start the action again. Kitty will be ready for more, pouncing and swatting at the frozen puck while you flick it back at him, feinting, checking, and scoring.

A final note: No high-sticking or high-clawing allowed.

Screen Savior

Let kitty worship the techno-gods on your computer screen — while you take an old-fashioned nap. This one doesn't require much human effort or interaction, but it's perfect for those inevitable moments when your cat is desperate for a good game of anything, and all you want to do is flop facedown on the couch. You've been praying for this one.

What You'll Need
- A computer with at least a 15-inch screen
- A variety of computer screensavers, available and downloadable online, from various cat-loving Web sites

How It Works
Point and click — yes, it's really that easy.

Set up an entertaining, eye-catching, mouth-watering screensaver on your computer, then let the software do all the work. Whether kitty's an old paw at Web navigation, a computer-cat newbie, or even a kitty Luddite, she'll sit for hours watching skittering mice, floating butterflies, wiggling fish, flapping falcons, or speeding shapes race across your computer monitor. Since most screensavers feature an ever-changing variety of dazzling eye-candy features, your kitty will be content to follow the action without ever laying a paw on your keyboard or — most important — demanding your attention.

CAUTION: You already know this, but cats have claws, and, yes, an overly curious kitty may scratch your precious computer screen. So wait and watch the first few times you try this one, and see if your cat is a computer mouser. If she goes after the image on the screen, you may want to skip using this game. But then again, computer screens are relatively inexpensive these days — maybe getting a good afternoon snooze is worth it.

Laser Sprite!

To humans, it's just a spot of intense red light that appears when we press a button on a pen-like device — but cats are clearly more imaginative than we are. A cat's mind and eyes transform that simple dot of ruby red into a magical, elusive fairy.

What You'll Need

- A laser pointer, available at most pet or office-supply stores (Tip: The office models last a lot longer. They're worth the extra money.)
- Room to run — kitty will need it

How It Works

Aim your laser beam at a wall or on the floor when your kitty least expects it. To get the cat's attention, create an audio signature that kitty will associate with the beam of light. You might try "Oooooh, it's magic dot time!" Fairy, fairy, fairy! or an eerie throat warble that will make any cat's ears twitch with excitement. Then move the light past your cat, making sure he sees it. Pounce! Kitty will be up and running, leaping for the ceiling or bouncing off the walls, trying to trap the beam of light that's always, maddeningly, just beyond his grasp.

Make your laser sprite climb the walls, dance on the ceiling, or scamper across the floor. Kitty will be in hot pursuit, and, yes, he'll get a workout.

CAUTION: Those laser beams can damage animal or human eyes. Never point the beam at anyone — cat or person — and keep the beam well away from pouncing, dashing cats.

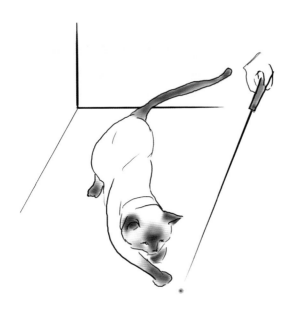

Tunes for Cats to Groove On

Ladies and gentlemen, kittens and cats, we're delighted once again to present the sophisticated jazz stylings of the original Bird.

So put your paws together for the Common Great-tailed Grackle.

What You'll Need
- A selection of audio CDs of bird calls and bird songs
- A CD/DVD player, a smart phone, or a tablet device
- One or more really cool cats
- CDs or apps that feature bird songs

How It Works

This is another semi-passive activity that will nevertheless intrigue and delight (and perhaps drive a little wild) your nature-loving indoor kitty.

First things first: You'll want to download or acquire several audio CDs of bird sounds. These are available on a multitude of Web sites devoted to the bird lover.

Next, pop in the CD, turn it on, and wait for kitty's reaction. She may rush to the windows or run around, looking for her feathered friends. They may be waiting for her — outside (sorry, kitty, you're out of luck) — but their sounds will be filling the house, so she'll keep looking.

Your cat may find one sound more alluring than another, so try a few and see what bird songs turn her on. Your cat may also fall asleep and simply ignore the sounds. If this occurs, rest assured, kitty will be dreaming of beautiful, elusive birds flitting and fluttering in her yard, outside her living-room window.

Leather-Glove Tickle

This neat trick will take your cat by surprise, especially if she's used to treating you to one of her sneak-attack, claws-out death grips.

What You'll Need
- Leather work gloves
- A cat with claws
- An ounce of courage

How It Works

Wait for kitty to roll onto her back. Slip on your thick leather gloves and purr softy to your cat, "Oooh, what a sweet little kitty. Does Precious want a belly rub?" Sure, play dumb. It's not hard for us. Let's face it, we're only human.

Or you can start the action if you want. Soften kitty up with some nice (gloved) belly rubs, maybe when she's on her side, snoozing in the evening.

Either way, she'll be playing possum, of course, ready to spring her Venus-fly-trap claws, but this time you've got protection. When she closes the trap, you won't feel a thing (remember, use thick leather gloves), and she'll really be able to dig in with her claws, which, apparently — due to her innate huntress-killer instinct — is incredibly satisfying.

One note: Cats may get sick of this trick once they catch on.

MouseStickle

This game provides a little variety from the usual mouse-toy games (tossing or string pulls), and it lets you keep a safe distance from your piranha cat's switchblade claws and teeth.

What You'll Need

- A sturdy stick
- Two to three feet of nylon fishing line
- A plump, plush mouse or two

How It Works

Wrap the nylon fishing line around the mouse tightly; then attach the line to the stick. Wait until kitty is on her back, and dangle the mouse in front of her. If she's not interested at first, drag the mouse across the floor, using your stick. The thin nylon line creates the illusion of a mouse on the loose, and most cats will take the bait. After a few passes, even the most aloof kitty queen will be unable to resist.

Now bounce the mouse up and down, grazing kitty's belly, and if she's sitting up, she'll probably flop over once the game begins. Your cat will enjoy swatting at the mouse and then kicking and grabbing it once it's in her hot little claws. As she holds on, gently pull the stick up and try to get your mouse back.

It's fun playing a little tug-of-war with your MouseStickle, even if you never win.

The Elusive Peacock Feather

No, you don't need to raid the local zoo at night. You can buy these long, colorful feathers from a local pet store for about a buck apiece. The idea is that you tantalize your cat — your cat clutches the feather in his claws. Not rocket science, but so what? Your cat's not a physics major, is he?

What You'll Need
- Several peacock feathers
- A standard intolerant cat

How It Works
Use your peacock feather to tickle kitty's belly and nose, or try wiggling the feather under a chair or popping it out from behind a doorway. These feathers are easy to move, and if you shake them quickly and let them rest, they seem to mimic the movement of prey that's cleverly hiding. Cats love to pounce on these feathery things, and they enjoy pawing at them while on their backs.

We usually sit in a chair when we're using this toy and tickle our cat's stomach. Forrest, our cat, loves to hate these things, and he can't resist swatting them and trying to grab them.

The long feathers tend to shred pretty quickly and break in half — but they do provide good cat fun anytime you use them. And for only a dollar or so, you can easily replace one.

Volleyball Smackdown!

A variation on the swat-themed games, Volleyball Smackdown lets kitty have a go at stuff with her paw and get supreme catisfaction from delivering a solid, well-timed smack!

What You'll Need

- A good variety of small cat toys and balls (Ping-pong balls are ideal, as are — for the oenophile cat — a wine-bottle cork. Our cat loves to whack corks out of the air, even when he's sober.)
- A "net" barrier that you create out of a cardboard box or a soft cushion

How It Works

Set up a little barrier that will serve as your volleyball net. A ping-pong table with a little net would be the ultimate court for this kitty game, but you don't need anything fancy.

Once you've gathered the players on the court, toss the ball up fairly high, so that it flies up and over the net. A higher toss works best for this game since it allows your cat to follow the ball in the air and get set for the smackdown.

The object of this game can be to keep the ball in the air as you hit it back and forth across the net. But what cats seem to like better is smashing the ball out of the air once you toss it to them.

If you manage to hit the ball and keep it aloft, well, score one for you. But cats, with their quicksilver reflexes and accurate aim, usually swat the ball down and over the net before your sluggish human responses can manage a save.

Prepare to lose.

Pitch 'n' Catch

A fun ball game for your all-star cat, designed to play with soft toys only.

What You'll Need

- A large array of soft, stuffed toys, suitable for tossing
- A cat with claws

How It Works

Keep kitty on a level playing field, sitting on a chair or table. Assemble a good selection of soft toys. Use anything with a little weight to it that will sail enticingly through the air.

Gently lob the toy toward your cat. The toy arcs through the air, and kitty tries to catch it. Cats love to snag the soft toys on their claws (usually impossible when you're tossing corks and ping-pong balls). Chances are, though, they won't play catch and release, so don't expect a toss back.

The rules? Cat makes a catch — cat wins. See how many catches he can make in a row.

Depending upon your cat's mood, he may choose to swat the ball back to you. No matter — let your cat decide. The object is to have fun, so enjoy whatever game your kitty's in the mood for.

Who knows? At the end of the season, he might win the Golden Paw Award.

THE GREAT (SAFE) OUTDOORS

Why do warm, secure, well-fed kitties constantly insist that they want to go outside? We, their devoted human slaves, provide them with good food, cozy beds, back rubs, foot rubs, belly rubs, and brushings. We set them up with kitty condos, kitty beds, kitty entertainment centers, and compatible kitty pals. Yet, they want to get outside, and if we — heaven forbid — ever leave a door ajar, our cats will be out cruising the 'hood, half a mile away.

Maybe romance is in the air. Maybe your little stud has been making connections behind your back (a bit of payback for that neutering visit to the vet), via Date-a-Tom.com. Hey, he can dream, can't he?

Blame it on instinct, boredom, or that deadly kitty trait: curiosity. Whatever the reason, your indoor cat will probably always be saddled with the inescapable urge to slip out of the confines of his safe, but somewhat predictable, indoor domestication.

How can we help kitties out of this fix (even if we've *had* them fixed)? Get 'em outside! It's easier than you'd think, and with a little patience, vigilance, and planning, you can provide a great, safe outdoor experience for your cat and not have to worry about the inherent dangers that do many outdoor cats in — speeding cars, coyotes, dogs, and owls, to name just a few.

Yes, you can turn your inside cat out — and you can do it safely. Read on.

Kitty Escapade with Harness and Leash

You might think your cat would never stand for this, but if you've got an indoor guy or gal who's itching to mingle with the birds and the trees, this activity is definitely worth a try.

We've been strolling outside with our cats for years — and once the kitties got past a brief, initial adjustment period, our daily harness-and-leash escapades have been as easy as, well, a walk in the park.

What You'll Need
- Thin, nylon, lightweight tethers to use as long leashes, available at most pet stores (The thin ones are usually sold for small dogs)
- A cat harness — also available at pet stores

How It Works
(1) Introduce your cat to the harness.
Be prepared: At first, your wary cat may not fully embrace your efforts. *No! Are you insane? You are not strapping that thing around ME, buddy!* So, begin the process slowly. Let kitty examine the harness on the floor: he'll sniff it, paw it, chew it a bit. These harnesses are made out of tough nylon straps or fibers; unless your cat's a Great White, chances are he won't do much damage.

When he's ready, gently slip one loop over his head. He'll shake it off, but try it again. Soon, he'll realize it's nothing to fear. At that point . . .

(2) Secure the harness around your kitty. There are two types of kitty harnesses you can buy: the double-loop style and the figure eight. The double loop has two fasteners — one for a loop which goes around the neck, and one for a loop around the belly. The figure-eight style is designed as one continuous piece with only one fastener. You adjust the size of the neck loop (the top of the figure eight) to fit over your cat's head. Then you secure the second loop (the bottom half of the eight) around kitty's back, fastening it under his stomach. Small plastic snaps (like the ones used on backpacks) lock the ends in place on both styles of harness.

At this point, kitty may freak out again (think bucking bronco in the O.K. Corral), but he'll get used to it pretty quickly. Praise him, and tell him how gorgeous he is wearing his new accoutrement. "Oh, Tuffy! Aren't you handsome!" Soon, if all goes well, he'll be strutting around the house, showing off his new outfit. Now it's time to . . .

(3) Attach the leash to the harness. When your cat's relaxed and standing still, casually sidle up to him and attach the tether to the little metal loop on the back of the harness. If you're careful and don't restrict his movement in any way, he won't even realize you've done it. Now let him roam around the house as you follow behind him, holding the tether up and away from his back. Just stay behind him, hold the lead — sort of like the queen's servant holding up the train of the royal gown. If you've been living with cats for a while, this is a role you're probably used to performing.

(4) Set some mini boundaries. Here's the skinny: You can't walk a cat. You can't make cats heel or stay. Not really. However, they will stop when they run out of lead, and it is possible to redirect them. So practice this on your walks through the house. Every so often, as you're marching along on your kitty parade, stop and let your cat realize he can't go any farther. Let him run out of tether and pull against the lead. Just stand there; don't pull back or try to direct him.

At first he will loathe, despise, or, at least, highly resent having this restriction placed upon him. But . . . he will get used to it. Try taking a step or two in a different direction, accompanied by the gentlest of tugs on the lead. He may get the idea he'd rather head off where you want to go — just don't try to force him. Gradually he'll get accustomed to the harness and leash and the idea of these gentle limits.

And when he does, you'll both be ready to . . .

(5) Head outside. This is an exciting time in the life of every cat and her human companion. Freedom, grass, and glory! Birds in the trees, sun in the sky, chipmunks and bugs to be eaten. As our cats tell us after returning from a good outdoor romp: It doesn't get much better 'n this! And you'll feel the same way, too, although you'll probably pass on the outdoor dining.

As with every step in this activity, you'll want to proceed through this one slowly. Never take your cat and simply carry her outside. Her first instinct will be to hide and run back inside the house. Instead, open the door and let her move at her own pace. Your job is to simply follow, holding the lead, and let her get her bearings. Caution and self-defense will be first on any cat's agenda, so give her all the space she needs — all you need is patience. If she wants to run back inside after a minute on the deck, fine — let her do it.

As kitty becomes used to the new environment, she'll want to go for longer walks. It's a good idea not to stray too far. Cats can easily become frightened outside; trucks, odd noises, kids on bikes — anything they perceive as threats will send them running. So beware: The last thing you want is to be a half mile from home with a frantic, panicky kitty.

Our cat walks are confined to our yard (which is fairly large) and short, half-block strolls down the street. We can almost always get back inside the house quickly if the cats decide to hightail it and run. But we've been caught off guard on a few occasions, with predictable results: tangled tethers, shredded arms, and hissing kitties.

Remember that cats count on their mobility as their first defense, and if they can t run and hide to protect themselves because they are on a leash, they'll be frightened and feel defenseless.

Finally, understand that you are not walking a poodle. I've yet to experience a "brisk walk" with my cats; they like to stop, stare, sit, and chew grass. Cat exercise usually involves some yoga stretches, followed by long moments of meditation. They are definitely not about jogging. So when you're outside with kitty and leash, try to become one with your feline. Enjoy the long, contemplative moments in the cool, fresh air. Let Mr. Puss stare at whatever he's decided to fixate on that day. You never know: You'll probably discover just how fascinating a twitching squirrel tail can be.

THE GREAT INDOORS

A surefire method for keeping your indoor cats lively and entertained is to create variety in their everyday environments. Something as simple as a wicker basket that had been occupying the far corner of the living room for years, placed unexpectedly in the center of your kitchen, can keep kitties intrigued for hours. *"How did"* that *"get there? Whatever it is, I have to jump inside it!"* An empty paper grocery bag, left open and standing in the middle of a room, generates a similar response and is another tried-an-d-true winner. Simple surprises like these are always fun, but you can also keep kitty entertained by creating environments that are a bit more elaborate than the old surprise-bag-in-the-hallway stunt. With a little imagination and some strategically placed items that will arouse a cat's interest, you can create mini kitty wonderlands that your cat will enjoy exploring for hours.

Tunnel of Love

What's better than an empty cardboard box just waiting for a kitty? How about several boxes, all lined up and taped together, filled with toys and treats?

Curious cats have to explore, and this easy-to-create kitty hideaway provides cats with a world of discovery. Of course, you can buy premade crinkle tunnels or similar toys for cats to jump into or crawl through, but why spend the money when you can easily make a hideaway yourself, using a few inexpensive, household items?

So start saving those cardboard delivery boxes you were going to recycle anyway, and put them to even better use. The Tunnel of Love awaits your adventurous cat!

And, yes, your kitty will love it.

What You'll Need

- Several sturdy cardboard boxes, large enough for cats to stroll through
- A few rolls of nontoxic tape (Beware: Some cats like to gnaw and eat this stuff)
- A box cutter or X-ACTO knife
- Ribbons and string
- Assorted kitty toys and tempting treats

How to Build It

Prepare your boxes by opening both ends and taping the flaps together, so you are creating a long, hollow square or rectangle from each box. If one end of the box is sealed and solid, simply cut away that section with your knife to open that end.

Once you have several boxes taped and ready, cut four or five windows on the tops and sides of selected boxes for kitty to look through. Use various shapes — ovals, squares, rectangles — to make these openings interesting little surprises for your cat.

Now you're ready to assemble your Tunnel of Love.

Begin by taping the boxes together, creating a strong connection by layering tape at the seam where the two boxes are joined. You can tape the boxes in a straight line — or you can angle them, using the flaps to create a bend that will allow you to snake your tunnel back and forth in a zigzag pattern. Some cats will enjoy the zigzag challenge, while others will balk if they don't see a straight passageway — experiment and find out what works for your kitties.

As you join the boxes together, tape some strings and ribbons to the seam area, allowing them to dangle inside the tunnel. You can tape more of them — or some peacock feathers — outside the cutout windows, so they drape across the openings. Tie a few toys to the strings and ribbons, which your cat will discover as she makes her way through the tunnel.

Once your tunnel is assembled, it's time for your cat to play.

How It Works

Introduce kitty to the tunnel, and let her sniff around and explore it. She may want to dive right in, or she may be a trifle cautious. Let her take her time. She'll probably find her way inside the tunnel eventually, but you can also encourage her by tossing a toy or treat inside or wiggling one of the ribbons, toys, or peacock feathers which you've taped onto a cutout.

Once your cat is inside, jiggle the strings and ribbons to keep the toys moving, enticing her farther into the tunnel. She'll also discover the cutouts and want to pop her head in and out. This is a good chance to use a peacock feather again. Wiggle it inside the tunnel from either opening at the ends, or use the cutouts for the same tantalizing purpose. You can also try running your fingers and nails across the surfaces of the boxes. (Fingernails sound a lot like little mice feet — so keep them moving.)

Some cats stay in these tunnels for hours — they're good hideouts — while other cats like to run in and out, thrilled with the adventure. Set up your tunnel in a spot where she normally strolls when she makes her daily rounds through the house.

Your kitty won't mind the morning commute to her food dish anymore, now that her route includes an exciting trip through the delightful Tunnel of Love. *Beep! Beep!*

African-Safari Theme Park

"In the jungle, the mighty jungle, the lion sleeps ..."

Let kitty discover his inner lion as he stalks the wilds of this indoor jungle maze, which you can setup in minutes anywhere in your home, and dismantle just as quickly.

What You'll Need
- Potted plants and pots of kitty grass
- Cat toys and other intriguing items
- Large stuffed animals
- Catnip
- Cat treats

How It Works

Before creating the kitty jungle, wait until your young lion is catnapping, dreaming of stalking marauding moles through his backyard savanna. Then choose a space that has enough room for you to set up your plants, grass, and hidden surprises. A basement is a good choice (since plants may tip over), but any room will do, as long as you're prepared for the possibility of sweeping up a little potting soil.

Begin with the jungle foliage: use thick, leafy houseplants and plants with long, waving grass (lemongrass, oat grass, and indoor cyprus plants work well and are inexpensive). Create a pathway, lined with plants, from one end of the room to the other. Place the plants fairly close together, but allow some room in between the pots, so your bold hunter can slip in and around the leaves and grass. Mix in some long cat grass (kitty will need green energy food for his safari adventure), and you've got your jungle! The more plants you add, the denser the forest and the more interesting the maze, but the number and types of plants you use are, of course, up to you.

CAUTION: There are many plants that are toxic to cats. Organizations like the Cat Fanciers' Association — http://www.cfa.org/articles/plants.html — offer much useful information on the subject. Find out which plants to avoid before investing too much effort and money in your jungle.

Once you've created your grassy maze, it's time to add some surprises for your jungle cat. Hide toy mice and treats among the plants, along with catnip sacks, small plastic balls, and other kitty favorites. Tuck the toys and treats behind pots and under leaves. Cats have a great time wandering through the foliage, chewing on grass, and uncovering all the exciting things you've hidden.

Finally, add a couple of kitty-sized stuffed animals to give Leo Jr. a little faux competition. Stuffed tigers, lions, cheetahs, and chimps — craftily hiding behind large plants and grass — will keep kitty on his toes as he stalks through his indoor forest.

When everything's ready, it's time to wake kitty so he can begin his expedition. All his big-cat dreams will be fulfilled as he explores his mighty indoor jungle. As he begins his safari, play a little background music for inspiration (don't all cats love Pete Seeger and the Tokens?), and kitty will be off and hunting!

"Wimoweh!"